Love Found Me

A collection of imperfect poems, about the perfect Love that found me.

Shalveeta Pareira

BookLeaf Publishing
India | USA | UK

Made with ❤ on the BookLeaf Publishing Platform
www.bookleafpub.in
www.bookleafpub.com

Dedication

To the broken, the lost, the searching.
May these words lead you to the only Love who never fails.
And may your story, like mine, begin again.

Preface

This book is for the teenagers searching for love.
For the ones who feel unseen, unchosen, and unheard.
It's for the lost adults who feel like life moved faster than they did.
For the ones who feel like they've lost more than they've ever gained.
It's for the backbenchers. The scapegoats.
The black sheep of the family.
It's for the adults who once believed they'd be living their dream by now,
but find themselves stuck, tired, and wondering if they missed it.
It's for the ones who feel like life has stolen too much,
your joy, your smile, your years.
It's for the people who love hard, give much,
and feel empty more often than they admit.
It's for the messy hearts like mine,
the ones who don't have the confidence to set the world on fire,
but still wake up and try.
It's for the overthinkers. The over-lovers. The over-assumers.
For those who wear their heart on their sleeve and wonder if anyone sees it.

It's for the ones who've felt misunderstood,
who've believed the lie that they will never be truly loved.
It's for the ones who are still fighting, still stumbling forward, still becoming.
It's for the one who's fallen, failed, and forgotten who they are.
It's for the heart that knows shame more than freedom, silence more than song,
and still dares to hope there's beauty left to be found.
I've always been a lover of words.
But more than that, I've become a lover of the Word – Jesus.
The One who met me at rock bottom.
I've wrestled with identity, comparison, loneliness, disobedience, and fear.
I've walked through seasons where pain spoke louder than hope.
But He pursued.
He restored.
He carried me when I couldn't carry myself.
And now, I write to tell you:
He is real.
He is near.
He is not done with you.
This book isn't perfect. Not even close.
Just like me. Just like my life.

I didn't write this to sound poetic or polished.
I didn't care about perfect rhymes or flawless grammar.
I cared about one thing: sharing the Love that saved me.
This isn't about me.
It's about a perfect God.
I never planned to write this book.
It came in the middle of my mess when I felt useless and helpless.
And I don't know the reach or the reason,
but even if this book finds just one person and whispers the love of Jesus to them,
it will have been worth every tear and every page.
You'll walk through three seasons in these pages:
Struggle Hope Becoming
This isn't just a poetry book.
It's a testimony, My Testimony.
A collection of moments where I thought I was too lost, too broken, too far gone
and yet, Love found me anyway.
So wherever this book finds you
whether in a tear-soaked midnight moment, or a quiet morning prayer
I pray these words become a mirror for your healing,
a reminder of His heart,
and a whisper that says:
You are not too far gone.
You are not disqualified.

You are still deeply, endlessly loved.
The same Jesus who calmed storms and healed lepers is still moving today.
In my life. In yours.
Your story isn't over.
God is not done with you.
God is not done with me.
God is not done with us.

Welcome to the journey.

And before you turn to the first poem,
let's whisper a prayer together:

Abba Father,
As I go through these pages, reading about Your goodness,
speak to my heart.
Holy Spirit, move.
Reveal to me the things that need to be revealed.
I surrender my life, my weaknesses, and all of me to You.
Take me, Lord.
Use me, Lord.
Make me usable, and help me build Your Kingdom here on earth.
Speak to me, Jesus.

Heal me.
Shape me.
Remind me that I am Yours.
Thank You, Jesus.
I love You, Jesus.
Amen.

"But the Advocate, the Holy Spirit, whom the Father will send in My name, will teach you all things and remind you of everything I have told you."
— John 14:26

Acknowledgements

First and foremost, Thank You, Jesus. The One who found me, saved me, healed me, and gave me a new story to tell.

To my family, thank you for standing by me through my darkest days, for forgiving me, and for still choosing to see the best in me. A special thank you to my mother, your prayers carried me when my strength ran dry. To my grandparents, sister aunty, and especially my Godfather, your love, faith, and quiet strength have shaped me more than words can say.

To all the people who left, friends I once called home; thank you. Your absence made space for growth.

To the friends who stayed and the ones who've arrived, thank you for filling my life with laughter, light, and hope.

To the many people I've met along the way, who watered my growth and believed in me even when I couldn't see it myself, your kindness will forever be written on my heart.

To the priests who came into my life like angels; Father Samuel, Father Ivan, and many others.. thank you for helping heal parts of me I thought would stay broken.

A special mention to Deacon Ivan. Your presence, your prayers, your love, and your unwavering support have left an eternal mark on my life. I will always be grateful for you.

To DYC and St. Anthony's Youth, thank you for the early opportunities and for being the foundation that helped me find my way back.

To Tabor Ministry, thank you for being a place of encounter and healing.

To the spiritual counsellors who stood in the gap and became vessels of His Word and wisdom, thank you for showing me light when all I saw was darkness.

To Sneha, thank you for showing me the love of Jesus in ways you may never fully realize.

To Saniya, your quiet love and kindness have touched me more deeply than words could express.

To everyone who hurt me, cheated me, abandoned me, or spoke ill of me, I thank you too. God used even the pain for purpose. Without you, I wouldn't have become who I am today.

To every person who prayed for me in silence, fought for me when I couldn't, and believed in me when I had lost all hope, thank you, from the deepest corners of my heart.

To everyone who has helped me in any way, shape or form. Thankyou for believing in me and helping me grow.

To you – the one holding this book. Thank you for picking it up, for allowing me to share my story, and for giving my words a place in your heart.

And last but not least, thank you, Me, my past self.

For not giving up. For holding on. For daring to heal. For choosing to try, again and again.

1. My Lover

I have a lover who loves me
More than I could ever comprehend.
A lover whose love knows no condition,
Is patient, kind, and soft to the end.

I have a lover whose presence feels safe,
Who stands by through all my highs and lows.
He doesn't seek but freely gives,
Never asks but always bestows.

His love is patient, quiet, kind,
Like a whisper that waits, not a voice that demands.
My lover knows me inside and out,
Knows me better than I know myself.

He waits to see me, to hold me close,
This one who is love himself.
My lover sees the mess, the mood swings,
The midnights of doubt and still stays.

My lover doesn't seek to take, he lives to give.
I hide, yet he knows exactly what I need.
My lover knows me; the hidden thoughts, the loud ones

too.
He knows when I run, he knows when I'll fall and he waits.

My lover wants to see me shine,
Always cheering from my corner.
Faithful when I wander,
Patient when I'm a mourner.

He listens when I break, he listens when I call,
Catches me when I fall.
And when the world dims,
He gives me light to fight my fight.

He spoils me with things that truly matter,
Gives me a glow like nothing else can.
My lover died to give me life—
A brutal death for me to have a beautiful life.

A true gentleman in every way, y'all,
My lover is the very best
And let me tell you who he is after all.
He's no ordinary man.
He is the very definition of love.

And his name... is **Jesus**

2. My Jesus

Jesus. Yeshua. Yahweh.
His name rolls off my tongue
Like honey, like healing, like home.

Soft is his voice, gentle is his touch.
His burden light, his yoke so easy,
Bright is his smile that means so much.

Eyes so beautiful that everything fades away,
Beyond description, too marvelous for words.
You can't comprehend him, can't understand him,
Greater than all kings, yet gentle as birds.

Big and great, yet tender and sweet,
Mighty and powerful, yet loving and humble.
His is the name above all other names,
Before him, every other power must crumble.

His name saves, heals, redeems, renews,
Brings the dead to life with just a word.
The sweetest sound to ever grace my ears,
The most powerful name that's ever been heard.

His name makes the devil flee in terror,

I stand in awe, completely undone.
What did I do to know this kind of love?
To experience this grace from God's own Son?

He is Jesus, My Jesus,
And let me tell you about ***My Jesus...***

3. Until I Met Jesus

Broken, bitter, lost was I,
Seeking love, seeking something.
I ran from pain but found it first,
Chased love with heart open wide.

I poured myself into empty hands,
Laid my body on empty beds,
Only to break like shattered glass,
Tossed away like a broken vase.

I drowned my shame in bitter drinks,
Found freedom in that nicotine,
Let strangers tell me who I am,
While in the mirror stood a hollow girl.

Too tired to stand or even live,
I thought I was easy, loose, and lost.
I gave myself away, believing
Being used was better than being alone.

Fake love, fake care, fake everything,
Same story, new soul,
Going around in circles asking:
Will I ever truly be loved?

Until I met Jesus...

He took my shame away,
Clothed me in dignity and purity.
Like the Samaritan woman at the well,
I was given a new life, a new story.

Jesus didn't condemn me,
Nor did he use me,
Nor did he question me.
He healed and renewed me.

Washed me clean in holy elixir,
Made me white as milk,
Dressed me in cloth from heaven,
And told me:

"You are my daughter,
Made in my image and likeness.
I have plans and purpose for you.
You are mine—
Perfect and fine,
Do not whine,
For I am the living wine,
Here to make your life sublime."

4. What Is Love?

What is love?
Gifts? Sweet talking? Touch?
Butterflies? Hugs & kisses?
Cute dates? Love letters?
What is love?

I never knew what love is
and I tried searching for it everywhere.
I thought the more love I give
the more I will receive;
only to realize it was never reciprocated.

Trying to find love in boys, men, things, world;
I tried to earn love;
through looks,
through laughter,
through late nights,
through ever after.

When I opened myself up
they were shocked.
I would cry in front of partners who never cared.
I opened myself up in front of eyes
filled with lies

and arms that had selfish motives.

All I needed was someone
to see me, accept me, hear me, love me;
just as I was,
for who I was.

Until I met a man named *Jesus*
who'd loved me all along.
He didn't need me to perform,
didn't flinch when I cried.
He saw my ugly,
and still chose to die.

Everything changed.
He loved me first,
He loved me all along.

My standard changed,
my heart changed,
my desperation was gone,
my loneliness flew.

He loved me;
even when I hated Him,
and didn't know Him,
even when I left Him,

and betrayed Him.

He saw the ugly me,
the worst me,
the lost me,
the broken me,
and He still loved me.

He cared about what I said,
and He cared when I cried.
He cared.
He saw in me what everyone dismissed in me.

He loves me.
He loved me.
And I still don't understand what love is—
but I know who love is,
and *He is Jesus.*

I no longer search for love in men or empty promises,
because I have found the love that is everlasting,
His name is Jesus.

I am now known,
seen,
loved,
appreciated,

celebrated,
and so so so sooo loved.

This love I can't explain,
This love I can't put into words.
This love I can never comprehend;
but all I can do is experience.

This love...
the love that is above all—
the love of Jesus.

5. You Are Who I Say You Are

They said my name with laughter,
A yoke, a stain, a shame.
I wore the whispers like a cloak,
Each word a growing chain.

But no one saw the silent cries,
The nights I begged for peace.
No one knew that deep inside
I only longed to be released.

They mocked me, spoke ill about me,
And tried to crush my soul.
Insulted me, called me names,
Their voices took their toll.

The insults grew so loud, so fierce,
I came to believe them to be true.
I started to see myself through their lies
And accepted them as truth.

Who was I? A loser? A slut?
A liar? A failure? A disappointment?
A curse? A SHAME?

A girl far too gone. Who was I?

And then I met *Jesus,*
And He said to me:
"You are not who they say you are....
You are who I say you are."

They call you names,
But I call you by your name—Shalveeta, My sweetest daughter.
You shine with grace despite their scorn,
Like light upon the water, with your crown.

They marked me too, they crucified me too,
They spoke ill about me too.
They pointed fingers at me too,
Called me sinner when I knew no sin.

So my dear Shalveeta, you are mine,
My beautiful daughter who I love beyond measure.
My love for you is deeper than the ocean,
Bigger than the mountains that stand.

I will go to any extent to love you,
To see your precious smile.
For you are not who they say you are—
You are who I say you are.

6. Stranger in My Own Body

Heart always beating outside my body,
Mind always racing beyond control,
Body always sweating, trembling, freezing,
Spirit always denying what should be whole.

I was a stranger in my own body,
A tenant in a house I couldn't recognize.
All I carried within was a heavy burden;
Fear like chains, anxiety my disguise.

The simplest tasks became mountains:
Brushing, bathing, rising from my bed,
Walking to the shop just next door
Felt like crossing oceans filled with dread.

I couldn't move, I couldn't breathe,
Paralyzed by what I couldn't name.
Was I cursed? Or was I truly cursed?
Two questions with the weight of shame.

"Why am I feeling all this?" I would whisper
To walls that never answered back.
Breathing felt impossible, lungs constricted,
Like something vital I would always lack.

Until Jesus breathed into me
And gave me a new breath of life.
His voice, gentle & sweet,
"You aren't cursed—you are blessed", child.

I have given you a spirit of power,
Of love, and a sound mind.
Not fear, not anxiety, not this trembling
These were never gifts of mine.

Leave your ways and come to me,
In me you will find what you seek:
Joy that bubbles from a deeper well,
Love that strengthens when you're weak,
Peace that passes understanding,
Kindness flowing outward free,
Patience, goodness, gentleness, faithfulness
These are my fruits you'll bear.

In your own body you felt like a stranger,
But I know you every cell, every breath.
Your Hair I've counted, Your name written on my palm,
Abide in me, and you'll discover what is calm.

And so He brought me, trembling still,
Back to my body,

temple of the Spirit—
My body, no longer a prison cell,
But sacred ground taken over by Holy Spirit.

His whisper, stronger than my fear,
"*Be still and know that I am God.*
You are mine, beloved and chosen,
No longer a stranger, no longer flawed."

7. The Search Ends Here

Yoga.
Kundalini.
Manifestation.
Crystals.
Rituals.

This tarot card reader,
that healer,
this guru,
that spiritual leader.

Loophole after loophole—
I kept spiraling,
searching for truth,
for peace,
for joy,
for a way.
For life.

It felt like a never-ending race—
to find *God?*
The Universe?
My higher self?
What was it?

"The crystals will heal you," they said.
"The cards will guide you," they promised.
"This energy will awaken you."
"This mantra will align you."
"This guru holds the light."
"This ritual will cleanse your karma."
"This breathwork will break the curse."

And so I ran—
in circles.
And circles.
And circles again.

Chasing light
in the shadows.
Grasping truth
in illusions.
Falling for wisdom
that left me emptier
than before.

Until.....Jesus walked in.
And just like He tore down the temple market,
He wrecked it all—
the idols,
the lies,

the false beliefs,
the fake escapes,
the counterfeit calm.

He looked me in the eye
and said,
"Girl, what you're searching for...is Me."
"I am the Way, the Truth, and the Life.
I am the Answer.
I am the Alpha, the Omega.
I am the firm foundation
you've been longing for.
I am the Living God."

And at the feet of I AM—
my searching ended.

Full stop.

I no longer chase.
I serve.
I serve ***I AM.***

8. Shalom

I wake up but I'm still weary,
Eyes open but the world feels blurry.
A thousand thoughts, a restless mind,
Trying to move but falling behind.

I count my failures like stars in the sky,
Each one a whisper saying, "Why even try?"
I kneel to pray but words won't come,
Just silence, just echoes, voices and feeling numb.

Tired of going around in circles,
Tired of myself and world.
I don't want this life,
I don't want to live.

Burdened by guilt and shame of yesterday,
Worry and fear of tomorrow.
Weary and broken and hopeless;
The only emotions I know.

Seeking for rest and peace,
Want it all no more.
Avoiding it all by mindless scrolling,
Eating and sleep.

I sleep all day, all long, all my life,
Hoping to escape,
Hoping to find an answer,
Hoping to put an end to it all.

Sleeping all day yet tired,
Weariness won't go ahead.
Seeking escape everywhere—
One YouTube video after another,
Doom scrolling,
One guru after another,
One instagram post after another,
Caught up in likes and fame.

All this until Jesus interrupts and says:
"Come to me all those who are weary and tired,
And I will give you rest."

My daughter, sit with me,
And I will give you peace
That surpasses all understanding.

Be with me, take my yoke,
Because my yoke is easy and burden light.
Sit with me, I will give you rest.
I will give you peace because I am peace.

'Shalom'— come to the fountain of peace,
River of calm and grace.
Sit by my side,
Lay your head on my shoulder and breathe,
And I will give you rest.

In my presence is where the rest is.
Shalom, My child
I am your rest

Shalom

9. Be Still

Voices I heard in my head,
Scary voices from all over–
"You should be dead"
"You are a curse"
"You are a failure"
"You are this, you are that..."

The screams in my head
Grew louder and louder
As I grew weaker and weaker.

Who were they?
Whose voices were they?
I would never know.

Every night, all day,
Every month without cease,
I would fight to stop them,
Desperate to run away.

I cried, I screamed for help–
Nothing. Nobody to help me.

What kind of storm was this?

Am I drowning? Am I dead?
Am I walking dead though alive?
What is this darkness
I do not understand?

I'm tired, so tired.
I can't take this anymore.

These voices I could never stop,
Never identify,
Until Jesus said, ***"Be still"***—
And boom, it all stopped.

"Be still and know that I am God,"
He said to the chaos.

In this storm, in my desperate attempt
To survive the battle between life and death,
I had forgotten someone named Jesus
Was in my boat all along.

One word from Him
And everything was calm and still.
One command from His lips
And the voices had no choice but to go nil.

In the silence that followed,

I found Him waiting,
Patient as always,
I heard Him speaking,
This is the voice I needed all along.

Be Still.

10. He Was There

When people I called family left,
He was there.
When I hated myself,
He was there.
When everyone abandoned me,
He was there.
When everything fell apart,
He was there.
When I wanted to die,
He was there.
When I was lost and broken,
He was there.
When I knew nothing at all,
He was there.
When my parents misunderstood,
He was there.
When I had no hope left to hold,
He was there.

I've run.
I've hidden.
I've turned away.
Yet He remained;
ever present,

ever waiting.

He was there when I held shame
like heavy chains around my neck.
He was there when I didn't even know Him.
In the cries,
in the pain,
in the doubts,
in the screams
He was there.

In the dark room when I was abused and used,
He was there.
When I sinned behind closed doors,
He was there.
In the evil man's embrace,
He was there.
When getting drunk and losing myself,
He was there.
When I lost my senses,
He was there.
When they tried to rob me,
He was there.
When they hated me without reason,
He was there.
When they misunderstood my heart,
He was there.

When I disobeyed,
when I lied,
when I cheated,
when I lost my innocence,
He was there.

Through doubts,
through confusions,
through confessions,
He was there.

Through ups and downs,
happy times and sad times,
cries and laughter,
mountains and valleys,
He was there.

He never left.
Not once.
Not ever.
He was there:
holding me,
leading me,
saving me,
guiding me,
teaching me,

protecting me,
loving me,
consoling me,
strengthening me.

He saw the cracks,
the doubts,
the scars,
yet He was there,
with arms open wide.

He never walked away.
Not once did He say,
"You're far too gone."

When I wept behind closed doors,
He was there.
When I smiled through pain at gatherings,
He was there.
When I made choices I regretted,
He was there.

He whispered truth while I wore lies.
He waited at the door of my heart
even when I pretended He didn't exist.

I thought I was alone.

But He was there.
Even in my silence,
even in my rebellion,
even in my numbness,
He was there.

Sometimes He was there as a father,
other times as a friend.
Sometimes as a healer,
other times as a teacher.
Through all stages and phases,
roles and circumstances
He was there.

Walking with me,
holding me,
sometimes picking me up in His arms.
Through it all,
He was there.

And now as I look back at my life,
I see He was there.
And as I look back,
I don't see my footsteps,
but a trail of His
When everything else faded away..
He was there.

He carried me when I couldn't walk.
He guided me when I was Lost.
When everyone left,
He was there.

My Jesus was there.

11. From Darkness To Light

My life was a mess,
my heart was broken,
mind clouded
and hope lost.

Demons inside me
crippled me with fear and lies.
All I saw was death
and all I wanted was death
nothing else. nobody else.
Nothing mattered.
Nobody mattered.

I wanted everything to end.
Wanted END.

Nights were scary,
people I hated,
self I wanted to kill,
truth I tried to find,
stories I tried to hide,
God I tried to find.

Who is he?

Where is he?

Jesus I had heard of but hated.
Jesus I knew but didn't really know.

Even when every ounce of me rejected,
a tiny fraction of me called out to him
with a tiny hope.

"If you are real, save me,"
I spoke into the air.
"Get me out of here."
"Prove to me you're God,
and I shall believe you
and call you Lord."

They said he is a living god?
Who knows.
This must be just another way
of filling and imposing religion.

I hated him & his people.
Yet in that hate,
anger,
rebellion
& disbelief,
I had faith like a mustard seed

and called upon him
again
& again.

and one day....
he answered.

And I knew he was a living God.
I knew Jesus is God.
The Saviour of the world
saved me,
found me,
met me,
and gave me a new life.

The life I wanted to finish
became the very life I wanted to live.

The person and God I hated
became the person I can't live without.

I hadn't met religion
but found relationship in Christ.
I had met *Jesus.*

Lord of Lords.
King of kings.

Way maker,
Promise keeper,
Miracle worker,
Light in the darkness.

He saved a wreck like me.

Jesus,
My Saviour,
Your Saviour,
Our Saviour.

12. How Did I Find My Love "Jesus"

I walked in carrying my grave.
I could no longer take it.
I wanted to "end" it
or give myself and life & God
one chance.

This or that.
One last chance.

Stumbled upon a retreat center called Tabor.
I went there,
walked in carrying my grave,
shame,
lies,
anger.
Walked in with zero hope
& hatred for all.

Nothing I wanted,
nobody I cared about.
All I wanted was some peace,
a place to breathe.

In the sea of believers
there was me:
an unbeliever,
a hater,
a traitor,
a rejector.

Days passed.
Nothing changed.
Nothing was felt.

But...
on the last day-
suddenly
I felt the freedom and peace
I had been searching for,
yearning for,
looking for.

And suddenly I could breathe better.
And suddenly I was free.
Suddenly I had come home.
That is when I knew:
I had met My Jesus

Jesus is God.
A living God

who met me
and transformed me,
an unbeliever.

That's where I had my *Damascus* moment.

And instantly I was home
and I knew:
Jesus is God.
A king.

Nobody who goes to the throne
will come back empty-handed.

At the throne,
every knee shall bow,
every tongue confess
that Jesus Christ is God.

This is where I found:
my God,
my answer,
my truth,
my love,
my lover,
and everything I was searching for—
Jesus.

And this is when I was given a new life,
one more chance.

Dead was brought back to life.

13. Still I Struggle

I've been so loved when I didn't know what love is.
I didn't know how to accept love
and I found Jesus.

But the old ways didn't change.
There was anxiety, fear, doubts, questions.
How can someone love me so much?
Why would someone love me so much?
How can this be unconditional?

The world was still as sweet as Jesus was.
God's love in the morning,
men's love at night.
Praises in the morning,
abuses at night.
Holy Spirit in the morning,
spirit at night.
Hope in the morning,
hopelessness at night.
Saint on the streets,
sinner on the sheets.

This was my life
even after I found Jesus.

Still, I struggle.
Still, I cry.
Still, I fail.
Still, I ask why.

Still, I fall into the same pit,
Still fight the same thoughts,
Still feel insecure,
Still doubt the cost.

I know he loves me,
But still I wonder
Am I enough?
Am I too broken?
Why can't I be consistent?
Why do I pull away?
Why do I love the world
Then cry when it fades?

Still I struggle with sloth,
With fear, with shame.
Still I long to be different,
But I'm stuck in the same.

Yet even in this mess,
He stays.

Even in this silence,
He prays.

"How can I leave the pleasure of the world behind?
God has made me to live and enjoy life.
I can't live a boring life with Jesus.
I can't let myself go.
No matter what I do he'll love me still
and won't let me go.

Until Jesus said:
"Being mine is what makes you- You.
Your identity comes from me."

And my brain was too small to grasp
and my faith was too little to accept
and I still struggled.

Yet time and again he revealed to me,
proved to me,
and time and again showed
that he is "God"
true living God.
A Saviour.

Yet even when I fail, he stays-close
closer than ever

saying:

"*Child, you're still mine. Even as you Struggle.*"

14. I Want to Come Back

God, I want to come back.
I've tasted Your goodness,
and I know You're good.
Not just in word,
but in the deepest parts of me,
I know.

I want to return
like I never left,
no mask, no shame,
just me,
like the prodigal son
running into open arms.
Father, I'm tired of pretending.

I want You.
I want to live like I know You,
walk like I've seen Your face.
Let my life sing louder than my lips.
Let my praise be in action
in the way I love,
in the way I forgive,
in the way I give.

I want to reflect You
mirror Your mercy,
carry Your kindness.
Let the fruits of Your Spirit
be evident in my every step.
Let them see You
when they see me.

I want to walk in
Godfidence and humility—
the kind that says,
"If He could save someone like me,
He can save you too."
Jesus, I want to be a living invitation,
a walking revival.

I've tasted the world,
and I've tasted You.
And now I know
nothing satisfies
like You do.
No drug, no gold,
no silver, no lover
can fill what only
Your presence completes.

At Your feet,

in Your embrace
I find everything
my soul has ever longed for.

Make me a light
in the darkness.
Make me a channel of Your peace
where there is hatred,
let me carry Your love.
Where there is injury,
let me bring Your healing.
Where there is hopelessness,
let me be the voice of hope.

Jesus, grant me the grace
to seek not to be consoled,
but to console;
not to be understood,
but to understand.

Make me a message.
A proof.
That light breaks through darkness.
That grace rewrites stories.
That hope breathes again.

I want to be an instrument.

Your disciple.
Your vessel.
Your living proof.

I want to come back to You,
not with guilt
but with boldness,
knowing I'm forgiven,
knowing I'm free.

No more shame
No more guilt,
because in You,
there is redemption.
There is healing.
There is purpose
in every scar.

You've forgotten my wrongs
and called me righteous.
You've forgiven me
and now I want to live
like I believe it.

Jesus is real.
Christ is hope.
Jesus is the living hope.

And even if my faith
is as small as a mustard seed—
I know,
You can still move mountains.
So here I am.
Not perfect.
But willing.
I want to come back to You.

15. Restored Path

I was once what they called a bright student,
an all-rounder full of dreams, full of goals.
"I want to be this, I want to be that."
Until failure & leisure came knocking at the door
& I answered.
Only to let the enemy in, to sweep me off the floor

Distraction & comfort became my best friends.
Hard work, dreams, goals
off went everything out the window.
Blinded was I, lost & comfortable.

SSC, HSC, graduation,
made it through it all
with zero drive, zero passion.
Lost in the lies of the world, making own plans.

"After graduation I don't want to work for anyone,
I want to do something of my own," I said.
No plans, no vision
just a pure way of distraction.

One job after another,
nothing I could stick to,

always showed up with lies,
false attitude, half heart & cries.

"I want to do something of my own," I said.
Sometimes a life coach,
other times a fitness trainer,
a healer and other times artist.

No vision, no goals.
Lost in the lies and illusions
& distractions of the world.

I never prayed or asked,
yet my Jesus heard my cry
and the desires of my heart
yet he knew what I wanted.

Unemployed I was,
hopeless for very long.
Comparing, crying, cribbing
my only job.

One fine day.
One yes to his call.
One step of obedience
changed it all.

I found my purpose & passion in emceeing.
Jesus gave me what I wanted
and suddenly I was earning,
doing what I love
& working for myself.

So many dreams now,
I don't know how to bring them all to life,
but I know Jesus is with me.
He is my CEO,
my provision,
my confidence
& he will make a way,
even if i don't know how.

He made a way when I had nothing,
gave me a platform,
resources,
opened doors,
and sent opportunities,
and made me something.

This is my Jesus.
Who says, "I have plans to prosper you,
to give you a life of abundance."

This is my Jesus.

A promise keeper.
A provider.

This is *Yahweh.*
This is *Jehovah Jireh.*

16. The God Who Doesn't Waste

Even when I fall short,
even when I doubt,
even when I do not know,
I serve a God that I know doesn't waste.
I serve a God who restores.

Yes, I think so much of my time I've wasted,
so much of my life I've wasted,
so much of my energy I've wasted,
so much I've wasted.
But I serve a God who doesn't waste.
I serve a God who restores.

Every tear, every pain,
every shame, every heartbreak,
every wrong turn, every missed opportunity,
every prayer, every cry,
every scream, every plead.
Years I fell behind,
wounds too deep to find,
the heartbreak, the shame,
seasons I even forgot His name.

My God doesn't waste-
He writes with broken pens
and paints with cracked palettes
and decorates a broken vase.

Like Joseph in a prison cell,
becoming second to Pharaoh.
Like Moses in the desert,
becoming a deliverer.
Like David among sheep,
becoming king.

Turning tests into testimony,
shame into story,
pain into poetry,
pits into platforms,
fear into faith,
loss into lessons.

I know I feel like I'm so behind
and I lost it all & wasted it all
my time, my energy, my resources, my life
on wrongdoings, things, people, circumstances.

But even in this defeat and disappointment,
I remind myself that I serve a God of deliverance,
I serve a God of restoration,

I serve a God who multiplies,
I serve a God who doesn't waste.

And when I ask & wonder:
"Did I ruin it all?"
He says:
"Child, I'll restore what you thought was lost.
I redeem what the locusts ate
and enemy stole
and people broke.

I am the God of Joel's promise;
'I will repay you for the years the locusts have eaten.'
I am the God of renewal.
I am the God of restoration.
I am the God of redemption.
I am the God that defeated death.
I am the God that lives.
I am the God that doesn't waste.

17. Walking Testimony

I am a walking testimony,
my whole life has been about
God's goodness, greatness,
favor & mercy.

All my life He has been faithful
& all my life He has been so, so good.
I've got miracles on miracles,
million little miracles,
so many miracles
that I can't count them all.

I've seen, experienced,
tasted, known God first hand,
yet I act like Eve in the garden:
saying Yes to the enemy,
doubting God's promise,
ignoring the truth,
seeking the world,
and falling.

I fall more times than I'd like to admit.
I falter more times than I can count.
I still question & I still doubt.

I still wonder & I still wander.

Like that one sheep
I keep losing my way,
I keep getting lost–
yet my Father so good
every time leaves the 99 to find me,
still loves me, believes in me,
and picks me up.

Even after getting healed by His touch,
I sometimes think Goliath is greater than my God.
I doubt God like the Israelites,
betray like Judas,
stumble like Abraham,
and disobey like Jonah–
failing to trust God that He will keep His promise,
failing to remember that He is a promise keeper
failing to remember that He finishes what He starts.

I still get anxious,
I still doubt,
yet my Father doesn't leave me
in fact, holds me tighter and closer.

I am not where I want to be yet,
but I'm on my way.

I've not yet become;
I'm becoming.
In my weakness, He is made strong.

My God is my good shepherd,
my God is my teacher,
my counselor,
my healer.

I still sometimes get lost in the world,
the distractions.
But the difference is-
I no more choose to stay in the dirt,
the pigsty,
but rather choose to get up,
shake off,
and come to my Father.

I'm not where I want to be
Still broken, still tired,
Still learning to pray
Instead of just hiding my fire.

Still battling comparison,
Still anxious in crowds,
Still figuring out how to speak
When my heart's too loud.

Not healed all the way.
Still have moments
Where my past holds sway.
But I'm not where I used to be.

I don't numb the pain anymore.
I don't seek love in lust,
Don't lie on cold floors.
I don't mask every scar.

Now I speak the name of Jesus
Out loud, bold, from the heart.

So no, I'm not where I want to be,
But I'm on the way.
And I know the Shepherd who leaves the ninety-nine
Will never let me stray too far.

The Father who runs to His prodigal child
Sees me while I am still afar.
The God who makes all things beautiful in His time
Is crafting my story with care.

I may stumble and fall,
but His grace catches all,
And His love is beyond compare.

I am a walking testimony—
Not of perfection,
but of His direction.
Not of my strength,
but of His redemption.

And I know God's not done with me,
So I'll keep walking today.

18. I Am Not My Mistakes

Yes, I make mistakes
but I'm not my mistake.
I fall more times than I'd like to
but I'm not my falls.
I trip, I stumble, I falter
yes, sometimes I don't know better.
Yet, I'm not my mistakes.

I've had a bitter past,
an imperfect present,
and face an uncertain future.
Still, I am more.

I am not the lies I once believed.
I am not the scars they left on me.
I am not the choices of yesterday.
I am not the doubts of tomorrow.

Like Peter who denied Christ three times,
yet became the rock of the church.
Like David who failed greatly,
yet remained a man after God's own heart.
Like the woman at the well with five husbands,
yet became the first evangelist to her village.

I am not the girl with anxiety.
I am not the girl that was once laughed at.
I am not the girl that feels behind in life.
I am not the girl that feels hopeless.
I am not the girl that once wanted to run away.
I am not the girl that raged at her parents
or was insensitive toward her sister.
I am not the girl that cheated, lied, disobeyed.
I am not that.

I am not my past mistakes.
I am not who I used to be.
I am not what I've done or where I've been.
I am not my past.

I am not bitter.
I am not salty.
I am not ungrateful.
I'm not my mistakes.

I am who God says I am.
I am who God calls by name.
I am His daughter, made in His image and likeness.
I am forgiven and not forgotten.
I am free & not a slave.
I am loved and not hated.

I am blessed & not cursed.
I am > I was.

"Therefore, if anyone is in Christ,
the new creation has come:
The old has gone, the new is here!"

I am clothed in strength and dignity.
I am fearfully and wonderfully made.
I am Chosen, Royal, Holy.
I am a masterpiece created for good works.

My identity is not found in my failures
but in the One who calls me Beloved.

My name is not "Mistake" or "Broken" or "Behind."
My name is "Daughter" and "Redeemed" and "Enough."

And no voice,
even my own-
can rename what God has already declared:
"You are Mine."

19. Even When

Even when faith is dry & prayers are cries.
Even when words won't come out of my mouth
& hands won't lift,
even when I don't get down on my knees
& I don't feel,
God hears me.

Even when I get busy doom scrolling,
even when my faith shakes,
even when the world looks more promising,
even when the idols take first place,
God sees me.

Even when the highs & joys of life
sweep me off my feet,
even when God seems too insignificant,
even when I'm busy,
God understands.

Even when I think I know better,
even when I put my faith in the world,
even when I jump into pits,
even when I open doors to temptation,
God saves me.

Even when I wander,
even when I go astray,
even when I know no way,
even when I doubt,
even when I question,
even when I give up,
even when I lash out,
God remains.

Even when I'm angry,
even when I'm sad,
even when I'm awake,
even when I'm sleepy,
even when I'm high,
even when I'm low,
even when I'm lonely,
even when I decide,
even when I choose—

God saves me,
God loves me,
God doesn't give up on me,
God rescues me,
God understands me,
God sees me,
God hears me.

For God is so good that He knows,
He knows my heart,
He knows my intentions,
He knows my why,
He knows my when,
He knows my standing,
He knows when I'm sleeping,
He knows my plans,
He knows my steps,
He knows my strengths,
He knows my weakness,
He knows.

Like the prodigal son who squandered it all,
still the Father waits, watching the horizon.
Like Peter sinking beneath the waves,
His hand reaches out before I call.
Like David in his darkest hour,
His presence never leaves the cave.

He knows,
and yet He leads,
yet He saves,
He forgives,
He loves unconditionally,
over and over again.

How good is His love,
how faithful with His promise.

Even when mountains crumble,
Even when oceans rise,
Even when darkness deepens,
Even when hope seems lost,
Even when I give up on Him,
He doesn't give up on me.

His love stands stronger than my doubt,
His grace runs deeper than my sin,
His mercy outlasts my rebellion.

This is the wonder I cannot explain:
That the God who holds the universe
Still chooses to hold me.

Even when....

20. What Is Faith?

Faith is what saves,
Faith is what heals,
Faith is what moves mountains,
Faith is what calms the storm.

What is faith?
Without faith you can't live life.
Without faith you can't know God.

What is faith?
Faith is the very thing
that got Israelites out of Egypt.

Faith is what helps you see the unseen,
Faith is what helps you move when you see no way,
Faith is when you see light in darkness,
Faith is when you find water in the desert.

Faith is seeing rain while the sun shines,
Faith is glimpsing mountain tops from the valley,
Faith is moving when no one else moves,
Faith is what makes you look crazy.
Faith is finding a way in the wilderness.

Noah built a boat when he had never seen a drop of rain
—
That's faith.
Abraham left home for a land he'd never seen—
That's faith.
Moses stood before a sea with an army at his back—
That's faith.
David faced a giant with just five stones—
That's faith.

What's crazy in one season
is faith in another.

Faith is unusual & without reason,
Faith is trusting something you can't explicitly prove,
Faith is the confidence of what we hope for,
Faith isn't just believing God can, but God will.

Faith is Godfidence.
Faith is Godvision.

Faith is Gideon fighting with just 300 men.
Faith is Esther approaching the king uninvited.
Faith is Daniel entering the lions' den.
Faith is Ruth following Naomi to a foreign land.

Faith was me trusting when I couldn't see the end,

Faith was stepping out when the path wasn't clear,
Faith was speaking life when death seemed certain,
Faith was finding joy in my deepest pain.

Faith is a lifestyle, a way of life,
Faith is trusting something higher and bigger than you,

Faith is trusting the driver when in a bus,
Faith is trusting the pilot when in a plane,
Faith is trusting the hairdresser when in a salon.

Faith is trusting the Author of your life,
Creator of you,
Driver of your destiny—
GOD.

Faith isn't the absence of doubt,
But the presence of trust.

Faith isn't having all the answers,
But knowing Who does.

Faith is the bridge between
where I am
and where God is taking me—

Not just believing,

but becoming.

Faith is knowing & believing that God who got me so far won't leave me stranded.
Faith is believing that my Story is Still being written.

21. Nothing Is Impossible

Nothing is impossible for my God,
Nothing at all.
I've seen Him do the impossible
over and over again since the beginning.

From bringing the dead to life,
From making the blind to see,
From making the deaf to hear,
From turning water into wine,
From feeding thousands with five loaves,
From walking on raging seas.

I know He is a God of the impossible.

My problems are big,
but not bigger than my God.
My worries are deep,
but not deeper than my God.
My doubts are strong,
but not stronger than my God.

I serve a God that parted the Red Sea
and defeated death itself in 3 days.
Then what are my little problems for Him?

Nothing at all.

My God is a God of miracles,
who makes the impossible possible.
I've got miracles on miracles,
a million little miracles,
I can't count the miracles in my life.

When a sinner like me was saved
a miracle.
When my sister was healed
a miracle.
When my sister, at the age of three, lay dying,
Doctors said, "We can't save her."
But God said, "She will live."
And she lives.

I've seen God work
in my father's life,
in my mother's life,
in my family's story.
Where darkness once reigned,
light now shines.
Where brokenness existed,
wholeness broke through.

When I was lost in new age darkness,

Depressed,
suicidal,
hating Jesus,
God found me, saved me, claimed me.
Now I'm a Jesus girl,
walking in light.

When work was lost
and doors seemed closed,
God made a way where there was no way.
New beginnings rose from ashes,
Blessed by the God who provides.

When I disobeyed and took the car out,
When things crushed and death lurked near,
God's hand
protected,
preserved,
saved.
I should have died-
but I lived.

Miracle after miracle,
I've seen it over
and over again.
The God of Abraham,
Isaac,

Jacob
is still the God of miracles today.

Your situation isn't as bad as it seems.
Your marriage isn't yet destroyed.
Your family isn't yet ruined.
Your health isn't yet beyond repair.
Your finances aren't yet beyond recovery.
You're not too far gone.
Your life isn't wasted.

Come back to Jesus
let Him write a new story,
A new beginning,
and turn it all around.

For the God who breathed stars into being,
can surely breathe new life into you.
The God who raised Jesus from the grave,
can resurrect your hope from the ashes.
The God who counts every hair on your head,
has already counted ways to save you.

Nothing
absolutely nothing--
is impossible for our God.

22. Walking The Narrow Path

I've met Jesus,
tasted His goodness,
known His power,
Heard His voice,
felt His presence,
hour after hour.
Yet the path remains steep,
the journey often tough,
The narrow road He promised,
would never be easy enough.

I forget sometimes
that I've been saved by grace,
I forget whose child I am,
whose image I embrace.
Life's storms rage fierce,
and difficulties mount,
I forget the victories,
the blessings I can't count.

When darkness creeps in,
I question and I doubt,
What my faith is built on,

what this life's all about.

I struggle
with gossip,
with laziness,
with pride,
With words
I shouldn't speak
and feelings I can't hide.
I still say things
I promised I would never say,
I still do things
that lead my heart astray.
My hands still reach
for what my spirit knows is wrong,
My mind still wanders
where it doesn't belong.

Yet in these moments of weakness,
when I stumble and fall,
There is no condemnation,
no punishment,
Only love that lifts me,
grace that sets me free,
And gentle conviction
guiding me to who I'm meant to be.

The fruits of the Spirit
love, joy, and peace,
Patience, kindness, goodness
that will never cease,
Faithfulness, gentleness, and self-control,
These are His gifts
to strengthen my weary soul.

I've not been given
a spirit of fear or shame,
But power, love, and sound mind,
in Jesus' name.
The armor of God stands
ready for me to wear,
A shield against the darkness,
a protection beyond compare.

So I rise again,
though exhausted I may be,
I rise to face the battles
that are set before me.
I rise because
the One who lives within,
Is greater than the world
and all its sin.

When the path seems impossible,

when I can barely stand,
I remember I'm held secure
in my Father's hand.

Walking with Jesus isn't easy
this truth remains,
But walking without Him
would bring far greater pains.

So I'll make
prayer my anchor,
His Word my daily bread,
I'll trust the Holy Spirit
by whom I'm led.

And though I may stumble
a thousand times more,
I know whose child I am
and that's worth fighting for.

23. Why, Lord?

Lord... why?

Why does life feel so heavy?
Why is just *living* so hard sometimes?

Why are there temptations pulling me in every direction?
Why does evil even exist?
Why is there so much pain and hate in this world?

Why is doing the right thing so difficult?
Why is there so much difference –
the rich, the poor, the strong, the weak,
the ones who seem to have it all, and the ones who have nothing?

Why is it always this constant fight
between good and bad, light and dark?

Why is everything changing so fast,
like I can't even catch my breath?
Why are there wars?
Why do people hurt each other for power, for pride, for paper?

Why are we so lost in comparison, conflict, confusion?

Why is there so much injustice, Lord?
Why do the innocent suffer?
Why do the guilty go free?
Why does death steal away the ones we love?

Why is it all so difficult?
Why does misery feel like the air we breathe?

Why does this world chase fame and money like it's the only thing worth living for?
What even is life, Lord?
What's the point of all this?

My little mind can't understand.
The truths, the lies, the noise, the pain, the purpose...
the philosophies, the theories, the arguments...
it's all just too much.

It's too much, Lord.
It's too heavy.

And even in this sadness,
in this anger, in these questions,
I see it –
my life is still a garden compared to the deserts others

walk.

You've given me blessings I never earned,
Mercies I never deserved.

I don't understand the world, Lord,
but I can trust You.

Because You saw this broken world too.
And You didn't turn away.
You stepped into it –
You wore flesh, You wore pain, You wore a crown of thorns.

You hung on that cross for every tear I cry,
for every question I ask,
for every war waged,
for every grave dug,
for every heart that breaks.

And You will come again.
You will make all things new.
The pain will end.
The wars will cease.
The questions will be silenced in Your glory.

So I'll wait, like a child;

small, confused, but still holding on.
With my hands lifted, and my heart wide open,
even when I don't understand.
Because You are still good.
And You are still God.
And You are still coming.

24. God Don't Give Up On Me

Part One: My Cry

God don't give up on me yet
I know it makes no sense but I'm trying,
Don't give up on me yet.

I know I've come so far, I've got so far to go,
But with this overthinking mind, weak body and scars,
I don't know how I'll make it through.

I feel tired, tired of this slow growth,
Tired when I fall into same old patterns,
Tired when I can't do what I want to do,
Who I want to be.

Lord, sometimes I think will I even get better?
Lord, why? Why am I the way I am?
Why is it so difficult for me to do basic things?
Why am I not disciplined? Why do I still act so immature?

I'm sorry. I'm sorry.
I'm asking for the answer.

It isn't you Lord. It's me.

Who is to be blamed Lord, you, me, or them?
When I look at others I simply feel so behind in life, Lord.
I feel so small, Lord.
I feel so defeated, Lord.
I feel so lost, Lord.

I wonder when will I become who I want to become,
I wonder when will I get better.

It sometimes all just feels so tiring
The anxiety won't leave me,
The overthinking won't stop,
The weakness gets worse,
And the will to live gets weaker.

In this armistice, this battle I fight,
Most of the times I lose and get knocked out.
I give up and give in and I ask WHY?

Why Lord, why?
Why am I so weak, Lord?
Why can others do it and I can't?
Why, Lord?

I call it laziness, I call it complacency,
I call it sloth, I call it lethargy,
I call it failure.

Ahhh....

25. God Don't Give Up On Me

Part Two: God's Response

But maybe, maybe just maybe...
It's all the lies I'm believing in
That's keeping me in circles,
That's keeping me "stuck,"
Feeling defeated and lost.

Because my God doesn't have a story of victim but victory.

Maybe I'm not weak, I'm not lazy, I'm not defeated.
Maybe it's a season,
It's a choice I've been making,
Or maybe it's the lies I've believed that aren't true.

Because my God doesn't talk of me the way I talk about myself.
My God can't make a mistake,
He can't create a loser.
Maybe I don't have to compare myself to others.

God is not done with me yet,

He will never give up on me.
His mercy is new every morning.
Maybe He doesn't want me to be strong,
Because He wants to be strong for me.
Maybe He doesn't want me to do it,
Because He wants to do it for me.

Maybe He's saying:
"Stop trying and forcing and surrender,
Lean on to me,
Your Daddy wants to help you,
Your Daddy is here for you."

I will guide you gently, softly, lovingly.
I will help you, I will give you strength.
I am not angry at you, I can never be angry at you.
Your struggle, your pain is my struggle and pain.
I want to help you, lead you—can you please let me?

Do not compare yourself, child, to them.
You know nothing about their life;
You know nothing about your own life, but I know.

I know it's going to be glorious and mysteriously miraculous.
Death will be brought back to life;
Darkness will turn into light.

I'm a God of the living and not dead.
I will give you strength that will never exhaust.
You will run and never grow weary.

My word will be a light and lamp to your feet.
I will lead you through the valley, deserts & mountain tops.
I will bring rains & shade.

I will provide manna in the desert.
I will part the sea for you and multiply the bread.
I will defeat the Goliath for you.

I will make you the head and not the tail.
I will bring you your Boaz.
I will make your paths straight.

Believe me, trust me, and let me take the driver's seat.

You aren't fighting against flesh and blood
But against the dark rulers & powers of the world.

Let my Spirit go before you
& fight the fight for you,
Teach you & counsel you.

Trust me.
I know the plans I have for you,
Plans to prosper you and not to harm you,
Plans to give you hope and a bright future.

I will never forget you or leave you.
You are mine.
I've carved your name on the palm of my hand.
Your life is mine.

I've sent you on earth for a purpose,
And I will fulfill that purpose.
All I need is a yes from you.

I will never give up on you
Because I love you too much to do that.
I didn't go on that cross to give up on you.

You mean so much to me,
You are so dear to me.

I take care of the birds and grass and animals,
Then how much more will I take care of you?

You are my everything,
You are my sweet little child.

I cared for you when no one did;
Why do you then think I'll give up on you?

I loved you even when you didn't love yourself;
Why do you then still question my love?

Even when the world turns their back towards you,
I will run to you.

I am for you and not against you.

You, you are my heart,
The apple of my eye,
My sweet child,
My loving sweetheart.

No matter how far you go,
How low you fall,
How high you rise,
How near you come

You are mine and you'll always be mine,
And I'll always be yours.
Nobody can separate us.
Nothing you do can make me love you any more or any less.

Nobody, nothing, no fire, no rain,
No enemy, no curse can separate me from you.

You are mine and I am yours.
I will never give up on you
Even if the world does, I won't.

I love you too much, so much.
More than oceans deep,
More than mountains high,
More than stars in the sky.

My love for you has no beginning and no end.

You are eternally mine,
And I am eternally yours.

26. He Just Wants You

I've used these same eyes
To watch things that grieved the Holy Spirit
And to witness sermons that stirred my soul.

I've used this same mouth
To abuse and curse
And to give praise to God above.

I've used these same ears
To hear lies and gossip
And to listen for His gentle voice.

I've used this same mind
To imagine wrong things
And to envision God's divine plan.

I've used these same hands
To hit and abuse
And to bless and help others in need.

This same heart has harbored hate and judgment
And learned to forgive and love without measure.

These same feet have walked into sin

And walked out through doors of redemption.

But what wrecks me—
What surprises me beyond words—
Is that my God's love never changed.

He still wanted me.
He still had a plan.

He didn't wait for me to clean myself up.
He is the cleansing.

Romans 5:8 tells us,
"But God demonstrates his own love for us in this:
While we were still sinners, Christ died for us."

That is not religion.
That is redemption and grace.

I know what He saved me from
And what He is calling me to.

If you feel like you're too far gone,
Let me be proof that grace runs deeper than guilt.

You don't have to be perfect,
Just a willing vessel.

My God didn't want me to be perfect.
He found me when I was at my worst:
When I rejected Him,
Hated Him,
Doubted Him,
Crucified Him daily with my actions.

He found me when I abused this body,
When I hated His children,
When I was drowning in alcohol,
Lost in sin and loving my lostness.

He found me broken, betrayed, abandoned.
He found me in the valleys, not the mountaintops.

He never asked if I prayed enough.
He never asked if I confessed properly.
He never asked if I was wearing my best
Or looking my cleanest.

He didn't care about my outer appearance,
But only my heart; which He wanted to make new.

He didn't care about my shame story
Or the stories others told about me.
He cared about writing a new story for me.

All He asked was:
"Are you willing?
Can you give me your yes?"

And He said:
"Come as you are.
I don't want a perfect you—
I want the real you,
The broken you,
The messy you.
Just you, as you are.
When you come to Me,
You need not clean yourself first.
You need not pretend.
You need not put on a show.
You just have to come,
And I'll do the rest."

If there's anything you learn from my story,
Let it be this:
God is infinitely bigger than our sin.
His love stretches beyond our worst moments.
His mercy makes a home in our weakness.

The miracle isn't that we find God;
But that while we were still running away,

He was already running toward us,
Arms wide open,
Ready to transform our brokenness
Into something beautiful beyond imagining.

He doesn't want your perfection.
He just wants You.

27. God In All

At the dawn as I wake up,
As the sun sets & light turns into darkness,
As the moon comes out and sun rises again
I see God.

In the flowers, in the sky,
In the birds, in the animals,
In the stranger's smile & baby that cries,
In the parent that loves & parent that frowns
I see God.

In the teacher that understands
& teacher that misunderstands,
In the mean boss and the difficult colleague,
In the friends that love and neighbors that give,
In the people that are for me and against me
I see God.

In those who hurt and those who betray,
In the clients that respect and clients that play,
In the well-wishers and naysayers,
In people that come to steal and people that come to heal
I see God.

In the friends that left & friends that stayed,
In the ones that drifted away,
In the fights that I lost and fights that I won,
In the people that helped and people that played
I see God.

In the laughter and in the cries,
In the joys and in the highs,
In the haters and lovers,
In everything that I earned and everything that I lost
I see God in all, I see God in all.

It's difficult to love, forgive, and serve,
And at times of weakness like this,
I remind myself that Jesus died for us all.
In the highs & lows I remember:
God's in it and God's with me.

Things won't work out my way always
God's way over my way,
God's will over my will,
God's timing over my timing.
Because I know God sees what I can't,
God knows what I don't.

Like Joseph in prison, thinking all was lost,
Like Moses at the Red Sea, nowhere to run,

Like Daniel in the lion's den, facing certain death,
Like Esther risking everything for her people

He works everything together for good
For those who love Him.

I trust that, I believe that.
It's difficult when everything seems to be falling apart,
When life is trembling, when you see no hope and no way,
When you feel like you're stuck
It's tough to do this life and do what's right.
This is where grace comes in, divine grace.

I don't want to live a life that is perfect,
But a life that pleases God.
Good or bad, I give Him praise,
When I stand and when I sit, I give Him praise,
When I lose & when I win, I give Him praise.

I praise in the valley, praise on the mountain,
Praise when I'm sure and praise when I'm doubting,
Praise when I'm outnumbered, praise when I'm surrounded
For praise is my weapon, praise is my hope,
Praise is my strength when I cannot cope.

Nothing is constant in my life,
Nothing is promised but only my God.
My God is constant—same today, yesterday & forever,
Who is faithful & true when all else fails.

So I will praise in the storm,
I will trust in the darkness,
I will hope in the waiting.
For the One who holds my life
Is the One who hung the stars,
Calmed the seas and conquered the grave.

In a world of endless change,
His love remains my anchor,
His promise my foundation,
His presence my peace.

28. When I Say, He Says

When I say "I'm tired,"
He says, "I'll give you strength."

When I say "I'm not enough,"
He says, "You're more than enough."

When I say "Nothing is working,"
He says, "I'm working out everything for you."

When I say "I can't do this,"
He says, "I'll do it for you."

When I say "I want to give up,"
He says, "Come to me, I'll give you rest."

When I say "I'm cursed,"
He says, "You're blessed."

When I say "I'm broken,"
He says, "You're becoming."

When I say "I'm ugly,"
He says, "You're the most beautiful child I've ever seen."

When I say "This hurts,"
He says, "I'll soothe your pain."

When I say "I can't take this anymore,"
He says, "I'll carry it for you."

When I say "I'm behind,"
He says, "I'm never late."

When I say "I missed out,"
He says, "You'll never miss out on what's for you."

When I say "I wasted everything,"
He says, "I'll restore it for you."

When I say "I'm in pain,"
He says, "I'll heal every wound."

When I say "I'm done,"
He says, "You've just begun."

When I say "I'm dead inside,"
He says, "Stand up and walk."

When I say "I'm lonely,"
He says, "I'm with you, always."

When I say "I'm a failure,"
He says, "You're a conqueror, winner, and victorious."

When I say "I can't,"
He says, "I can, through you."

When I say "It's too late,"
He says, "My timing is perfect."

When I say "I'm afraid,"
He says, "Fear not, for I am with you."

When I say "I'm anxious,"
He says, "Peace I leave with you."

When I say "I'm lost,"
He says, "I am the way."

When I say "I'm in darkness,"
He says, "I am the light of the world."

When I say "Nobody loves me,"
He says, "I love you."

When I say "I've gone too far,"
He says, "My grace reaches farther."

When I say "I'm worthless,"
He says, "You were worth dying for."

When I say "I'm forgotten,"
He says, "I've carved you on the palm of my hand."

When I say "I'm stuck,"
He says, "I make a way where there is no way."

When I say "I'm overwhelmed,"
He says, "Come to me all who are weary."

When I say "I'm a mistake,"
He says, "You are fearfully and wonderfully made."

When I say "I can't forgive myself,"
He says, "I remember your sins no more."

There is power in what He says.
In the beginning was the Word, and the Word was God.
The earth was created with His Word.
One word He speaks over my life can heal
And bring dead parts to life and let them shine.

His Word stands when all else falls.
His voice calms storms, moves mountains,
Parts seas, and raises the dead.

When the world speaks death,
He speaks life.

When I say "It's impossible,"
He says, "All things are possible."

And with that one word,
Everything changes.

29. Walking In Grace

I don't know where I'm going
or where I'm heading
or what's in store for me.

Some days everything feels possible,
other days everything is just so difficult.

Time waits for none, life waits for none,
and in this society we live in,
nothing is ever enough.

I have dreams
but how do I make them reality?
Some days I don't even know what I want.

In this uncertainty and fear of future
I remind myself of my history,
I am where I am right now
not because of my work or what I've done
but because of God's grace.

Every little detail of my life,
I've seen God's hand at work,
through school, through college, everything.

He continues to show me
that His grace will carry me.
So in this moment of not knowing,
I choose trust over uncertainty,
Faith over fear,
Hope over doubt.

The same grace that carried me yesterday
Will lead me through tomorrow's dawn.

Everything will find its perfect place,
In its perfect time.

I hold on to this hope
that things will continue to get better,
that it'll all be better than I can ever imagine.

It'll all work out
and I'll live a beautiful life.

And perhaps this is true for you too
Standing in your own uncertainty,
Remember that some roads reveal themselves
Only as we take the step to walk them.

Trust the unseen hand that guides,

The promise of a beautiful life unfolding.

We will both arrive exactly where we're meant to be,
Carried by grace, into light we cannot yet imagine.

30. God Is Not Done With Me Yet

I've seen death & I've seen life
I've lived in darkness & I've lived in light
I've lost myself & I've found myself
I've lived from shame to shame & glory to glory.

I've lived hidden & I've lived with eyes on me
I've experienced pain & I've experienced joy
I've tasted God's punishment & I've tasted God's grace
I've ruined it all & I've built it all.

I've wasted it all & I've restored it all
I've cheated & have been cheated on
I've loved & have been loved
I've lived without God & I've lived with God.

I know what is life without Him & with Him
I've done life with my own strength & will
I've done life surrendered to Him
I've seen tongues abuse & shame me
I've seen same tongues praise & lift me.

I've fallen down in front of people
God has lifted me up in front of the same people

I've lost it all & I've gained it all
I've seen tears of pain & ache
I've seen tears of joy & gratitude.

I've lived to take & I've lived to give
I've disobeyed & I've obeyed
I've tasted death & life
I've seen curses & I've seen miracles
I've seen evil spirits at work & I've seen Holy Spirit at work.

I am a living, walking, breathing miracle
A testimony etched in flesh and blood
I've lived a life I hate
I'm living a life I'm liking.

I'm not there yet, I'm getting there
I'm not complete, I'm becoming
I'm a puzzle in the making
God the potter who is molding and sculpting me.

I am not where I used to be
But I'm also not where I want to be
Not even close to it
But I'm on my way.

I've got stories that built me & broke me

Stories I'm proud of and ashamed of
I don't know what is next
I don't know where I'm going
I don't know how it's gonna unfold.

I've been carried by grace through faith
The story isn't yet written but in the writing
The movie isn't yet completed but in the making
I've seen divine at work in small & big things
In seen & unseen, heard & unheard.

I've experienced love & grace, support & applause
I've also seen downfall & hate
The journey is still on
I'm on my way—heaven is my destination
Holy Spirit my guide, God's word my GPS.

This isn't my end
I've seen God move mysteriously and miraculously
Too many times all my life
And I'm excited to see where I'm going
I'm excited to build & live this life with my Jesus
Who has never failed & will never fail.

I don't know it yet but it's all going to work out
It's all coming together, it'll all make sense
One day at a time with one prayer and petition

With worship as my weapon & praise my secret
With faith & trust with my arms open wide
& heart that is surrendered
I am walking, I am moving, I am becoming.

GOD IS NOT DONE WITH ME YET
He is not against me, He is for me & with me
I will make it because He always steps in
My God is in it, He is working through me.

Even when I'm against myself and temptations beat
Even when I feel His presence and when I don't
Even when I understand & when I don't
Even when I'm strong & when I'm weak
Even when I'm defeated & sick
Even when I don't feel like I'm able
Even when I want to give up.

My God will work through me
My God will fight for me
I have a power greater than all the enemy's lies
I know the truth of the gospel.

My God is with me
My God is by my side
This is not my fight, He is my defense
God holds my life

This is my confidence.

I won't forget all the great things He has done
I will never forget He's sufficient for me
I will never forget His promises
I will never forget my history.

My God is more than able
I put my trust in the One who still does miracles
He does miracles
My God is more than able.

I know who I am with
I know how far I've come
I know my God is able
And I can't turn back
But fix my eyes on Jesus and look forward.

There is so much more to my story
My God is not done with me yet
My Lover is not done with me yet
This love story continues to unfold
Each page written with His scarred hands.

This is my story. This is my song.
This is my life. This is my Lover.

Jesus and I, we're still writing our love story
And the most beautiful chapters are yet to come

31. All I Can Say Is Thank You

Thank You, Jesus, for never leaving my side.
Thank You, Jesus, for the stories yet to be written.
Thank You, Jesus, for not giving up on me.
Thank You, Jesus, for all that I can see and all that I can't.
Thank You, Jesus, for being my Saviour.
Thank You, Jesus, for being my best friend.
Thank You, Jesus, for saving me from death.
Thank You, Jesus, for giving me a new life.
Thank You, Jesus, for the hope that is found in You.
Thank You, Jesus, for Your grace.
Thank You, Jesus, for Your mercy.
Thank You, Jesus, for everything small and big.
Thank You, Jesus, for the strength to go on.
Thank You, Jesus, for the gift of Mother Mary.
Thank You, Jesus, for the gift of the Holy Spirit – my Guide, my Teacher, my Comforter, my Advocate.
Thank You, Jesus, for this life.
Thank You, Jesus, for the hurt and the pain.
Thank You, Jesus, for the good and the bad.
Thank You, Jesus, for everything in between.
Thank You, Jesus, for Your love.
Thank You, Jesus, for the safety that comes from You.
Thank You, Jesus, for all the surprises.

Thank You, Jesus, for all the things that bring me joy.
Thank You, Jesus, for Your provision.
Thank You, Jesus, for Your well that never runs dry.
Thank You, Jesus, for all You've done.
Thank You, Jesus, for You.
Thank You, Jesus, for giving Your life for me.
Thank You, Jesus, for the free gift of salvation.
Thank You, Jesus, for my faith.
Thank You, Jesus, for the gift of my life.
Thank You, Jesus, for my fight.
Thank You, Jesus, for my family.
Thank You, Jesus, for my purpose.
Thank You, Jesus, for my ministry.
Thank You, Jesus, for my talents and blessings.
Thank You, Jesus, for my heart.
Thank You, Jesus, for my abled body.
Thank You, Jesus, for all the luxury.
Thank You, Jesus, for the roof over my head.
Thank You, Jesus, for the clothes on me.
Thank You, Jesus, for the food on my table.
Thank You, Jesus, for my friends.
Thank You, Jesus, for my clients.
Thank You, Jesus, for everyone who loves me.
Thank You, Jesus, for everyone who wishes well for me.
Thank You, Jesus, for everyone who's been there to help and support me.
Thank You, Jesus, for the people in my life and the ones

who left.
Thank You, Jesus, for the people I've yet to meet.
Thank You, Jesus, for the story I've yet to tell.
Thank You, Jesus, for my future husband.
Thank You, Jesus, for my grandparents.
Thank You, Jesus, for the overflow.
Thank You, Jesus, for second chances.
Thank You, Jesus, for forgiveness.
Thank You, Jesus, for mercy that is new every morning.
Thank You, Jesus, for keeping Your promises.
Thank You, Jesus, for the angels and the saints.
Thank You, Jesus, for Your Word.
Thank You, Jesus, for the gift of Church.
Thank You, Jesus, for community.
Thank You, Jesus, for the seasons.
Thank You, Jesus, for nature.
Thank You, Jesus, for beauty.
Thank You, Jesus, for this life.
Thank You, Jesus, You set me free.
Thank You, Jesus, You rescued me.
Thank You, Jesus, You gave me a new life, a new story, a new reason to live.
Thank You, Jesus, for the dreams.
Thank You, Jesus, for everything that is coming and I've yet to see.
Thank You, Jesus.
Thank You, Jesus.

Thank You, Jesus.

Thank You is the only song I can sing.
Thank You is all I know to say.

Every time I think of You,
And all You've done,
My words fall short.

I have nothing new,
No way to measure my gratitude.

So here is all I have –
Thank You, Jesus.
I love You, Jesus.

32. To The One Holding This Book.

You didn't choose this book,
this book chose you.
And I'm so glad, so grateful,
that you're here.

I might know your name, or I might not
but that doesn't matter.
What matters is this moment,
and what I'm about to tell you.

I don't know your story.
I don't know your struggles, your silent battles,
the tears you've hidden,
the sleepless nights.

I don't know your wins or your losses,
If you're smiling for real,
or if you've forgotten how.

But here's what I do know:
There's a man named Jesus,
and He loves you.

He loves you so deeply, so fiercely,
that no poem, no song, no movie
could ever do His love justice.

He is not just my lover
He is yours too.

You were never meant to do life alone.
Not on your own strength, not in your own power.
There's someone waiting to help you,
to hold you,
to walk this journey with you.

All you have to do is let Him in.

Go to the altar,
where the Father's arms are open wide.
Forgiveness and healing were bought for you
with the precious blood of Jesus Christ.

He longs for a relationship with you
to walk with you,
to talk with you,
to carry what you can't.

He wants to lead you to a place
where milk and honey flow,

to give you wisdom more precious
than gold or silver.

He promises peace beyond understanding,
strength for your weakest days,
hope for the hopeless,
a future filled with purpose.

For once, try.
Try surrendering everything at His feet.
Try giving Him a chance.
Try letting Him in.

I've tasted His love,
and it's the most beautiful thing I've ever known.

I'm not perfect.
I fail – every day, every second –
but His love has never failed me.

I'm so glad you picked up these pages,
so glad you heard my story,
so glad you let these poems find you.

I hope they gave you hope,
and reminded you just how good,
how kind,

how great
our Jesus is.

And if my testimony moved you,
if it stirred something small inside you,

I invite you:
Give Him one chance.
One moment. One yes.
You have nothing to lose,
but everything to gain.
He's waiting for you.
He's knocking at your door.
He is for you.

Let His love find you.
Let His love transform you.
Let His love shine upon you.
Let His love guide you –
all the way home

9 789369 532919

Printed by Libri Plureos GmbH in Hamburg,
Germany